The Poetry of Bliss Carman

Volume XVIII - April Airs: A Book of New England Lyrics

TO THE ELIZABETHAN CLUB OF YALE UNIVERSITY WITH SINCERE APPRECIATION THESE VERSES ARE RESPECTFULLY DEDICATED

William Bliss Carman was born in Fredericton, in New Brunswick on April 15th 1861. He was educated at Fredericton Collegiate School before moving to the University of New Brunswick, obtaining his B.A. there in 1881. As is common with so many writers his first published piece was for the University magazine and for Carman that was in 1879.

After several years editing various magazines and periodicals Carman first published a poetry volume in 1893 with Low Tide on Grand Pré. There was no Canadian company prepared to publish and when an American company did so it went bankrupt.

The following year was decidedly better. His partnership with the American poet Richard Hovey had given birth to Songs of Vagabondia. It was an immediate success.

That success prompted the Boston firm, Stone & Kimball, to reissue Low Tide on Grand Pré and to hire Carman as the editor of its literary journal, The Chapbook.

Carman brought out, in 1895, Behind the Arras, a somewhat more serious and philosophical work centered on the premise of a long meditation, using the speaker's house and its many rooms, as a symbol of life and the choices to be made.

In 1896 Carman met Mrs Mary Perry King, who rapidly became patron, adviser and sometime lover. She also became his writing collaborator on two verse dramas.

In 1897 Carman published Ballad of Lost Haven, and in 1898, By the Aurelian Wall, the title poem itself was an elegy to John Keats and the book was a collection of formal elegies.

As the century turned Carman was hard at work on a five-volume set of poetry "Pans Pipes". The excellence of a number of these poems did much to install Carman as the most noted of Canadian Poets and eventually their own Poet Laureate.

In 1912 the final work in the Vagabondia series was published. Richard Hovey had died in 1900 and so this last work was purely Carman's. It has a distinct elegiac tone as if remembering the past works themselves.

On October 28th, 1921 Carman was honored by the newly-formed Canadian Authors' Association where he was crowned Canada's Poet Laureate with a wreath of maple leaves.

William Bliss Carman died of a brain hemorrhage at the age of 68 in New Canaan on the 8th June, 1929.

Index of Contents

APRIL AIRS

THE DESERTED PASTURE

I love the stony pasture
That no one else will have.
The old gray rocks so friendly seem,
So durable and brave.

In tranquil contemplation
It watches through the year,
Seeing the frosty stars arise,
The slender moons appear.

Its music is the rain-wind,
Its choristers the birds,
And there are secrets in its heart
Too wonderful for words.

It keeps the bright-eyed creatures
That play about its walls,
Though long ago its milking herds
Were banished from their stalls.

Only the children come there,
For buttercups in May,
Or nuts in autumn, where it lies
Dreaming the hours away.

Long since its strength was given
To making good increase,
And now its soul is turned again
To beauty and to peace.

There in the early springtime
The violets are blue,
And adder-tongues in coats of gold.
Are garmented anew.

There bayberry and aster
Are crowded on its floors,
When marching summer halts to praise
The Lord of Out-of-doors.

And there October passes
In gorgeous livery, —
In purple ash, and crimson oak,
And golden tulip tree.

And when the winds of winter
Their bugle blasts begin,
The snowy hosts of heaven arrive
To pitch their tents therein.

THE OLD GRAY WALL

Time out of mind I have stood
Fronting the frost and the sun,
That the dream of the world might endure,
And the goodly will be done.

Did the hand of the builder guess,
As he laid me stone by stone,
A heart in the granite lurked,
Patient and fond as his own?

Lovers have leaned on me
Under the summer moon,
And mowers laughed in my shade
In the harvest heat at noon.

Children roving the fields
With early flowers in spring,
Old men turning to look,
When they heard a bluebird sing,

And travellers along the road
From rising to setting sun,
Have seen, yet imagined not
The kindness they gazed upon.

Ah, when will ye understand,
Mortals, —nor deem it odd, —
Who rests on this old gray wall
Lays a hand on the shoulder of God!

BLOODROOT

When April winds arrive
And the soft rains are here,
Some morning by the roadside
These gipsy folk appear.

We never see their coming,
However sharp our eyes;
Each year as if by magic
They take us by surprise.

Along the ragged woodside
And by the green spring-run,
Their small white heads are nodding
And twinkling in the sun.

They crowd across the meadow
In innocence and mirth,
As if there were no sorrow
In al the lovely earth.

So frail, so unregarded,—
And yet about them clings
That exquisite perfection,
The soul of common things!

Think you the springing pastures
Their starry vigil kept,
To hear along the midnight

Some message, while we slept?

How else should spring requicken
Such glory in the sod?
I guess that trail of beauty
Is where the angel trod.

EARTH VOICES

I

I heard the spring wind whisper
Above the brushwood fire,
"The world is made forever
Of transport and desire.

"I am the breath of being,
The primal urge of things;
I am the whirl of star dust,
I am the lift of wings.

"I am the splendid impulse
That comes before the thought,
The joy and exaltation
Wherein the life is caught.

"Across the sleeping furrows
I call the buried seed,
And blade and bud and blossom
Awaken at my need.

"Within the dying ashes
I blow the sacred spark,
And make the hearts of lovers
To leap against the dark."

II

I heard the spring light whisper
Above the dancing stream,
"The world is made forever
In likeness of a dream.

"I am the law of planets,
I am the guide of man;

The evening and the morning
Are fashioned to my plan.

"I tint the dawn with crimson,
I tinge the sea with blue;
My track is in the desert,
My trail is in the dew.

"I paint the hills with color,
And in my magic dome
I light the star of evening
To steer the traveller home.

"Within the house of being,
I feed the lamp of truth
With tales of ancient wisdom
Anc prophecies of youth."

III

I heard the spring rain murmur
Above the roadside flower,
"The world is made forever
In melody and power.

"I keep the rhythmic measure
That marks the steps of time,
And all my toil is fashioned
To symmetry and rhyme.

"I plow the untilled upland,
I ripe the seeding grass,
And fill the leafy forest
With music as I pass.

"I hew the raw rough granite
To loveliness of line,
And when my work is finished,
Behold, it is divine!

"I am the master-builder
In whom the ages trust.
I lift the lost perfection
To blossom from the dust."

IV

Then Earth to them made answer,
As with a slow refrain
Born of the blended voices
Of wind and sun and rain,

"This is the law of being
That links the threefold chain:
The life we give to beauty
Returns to us again."

NOW IS THE TIME OF YEAR

Now is the time of year
When all the flutes begin, —
The redwing bold and clear,
The rainbird far and thin.

In all the waking lands
There's not a wilding thing
But knows and understands
The burden of the spring.

Now every voice alive
By rocky wood and stream
Is lifted to revive
The ecstasy, the dream.

For Nature, never old,
But busy as of yore,
From sun and rain and mould
Is making spring once more.

She sounds her magic note
By river-marge and hill,
And every woodland throat
Re-echoes with a thrill.

O mother of our days,
Hearing thy music call,
Teach us to know thy ways
And fear no more at all!

NOW THE LILAC TREE'S IN BUD

Now the lilac tree's in bud,
And the morning birds are loud.
Now a stirring in the blood
Moves the heart of every crowd.

Word has gone abroad somewhere
Of a great impending change.
There's a message in the air
Of an import glad and strange.

Not an idler in the street,
But is better off to-day.
Not a traveller you meet,
But has something wise to say.

Now there's not a road too long,
Not a day that is not good,
Not a mile but hears a song
Lifted from the misty wood.

Down along the Silvermine
That's the blackbird's cheerful note!
You can see him flash and shine
With the scarlet on his coat.

Now the winds are soft with rain,
And the twilight has a spell,
Who from gladness could refrain
Or with olden sorrows dwell?

THE REDWING

I hear you, Brother, I hear you,
Down in the alder swamp,
Springing your woodland whistle
To herald the April pomp!

First of the moving vanguard,
In front of the spring you come,
Where flooded waters sparkle
And streams in the twilight hum.

You sound the note of the chorus
By meadow and woodland pond,
Till, one after one up-piping,

A myriad throats respond.

I see you, Brother, I see you,
With scarlet under your wing,
Flash through the ruddy maples,
Leading the pageant of spring.

Earth has put off her raiment
Wintry and worn and old,
For the robe of a fair young sibyl,
Dancing in green and gold.

I heed you, Brother. To-morrow
I, too, in the great employ,
Will shed my old coat of sorrow
For a brand-new garment of joy.

AN APRIL MORNING

Once more in misted April
The world is growing green.
Along the winding river
The plumey willows lean.

Beyond the sweeping meadows
The looming mountains rise,
Like battlements of dreamland
Against the brooding skies.

In every wooded valley
The buds are breaking through,
As though the heart of all things
No languor ever knew.

The golden-wings and bluebirds
Call to their heavenly choirs.
The pines are blued and drifted
With smoke of brushwood fires.

And in my sister's garden
Where little breezes run,
The golden daffodillies
Are blowing in the sun.

THE SOUL OF APRIL

Over the wintry threshold
Who comes with joy to-day,
So frail, yet so enduring,
To triumph o'er dismay?

Ah, quick her tears are springing,
And quickly they are dried,
For sorrow walks before her,
But gladness walks beside.

She comes with gusts of laughter,—
The music as of rills;
With tenderness-and sweetness, —
The wisdom of the hills.

Her hands are strong to comfort,
Her heart is quick to heed.
She knows the signs of sadness,
She knows the voice of need.

There is no living creature,
However poor or small,
But she will know its trouble,
And hasten to its call.

Oh, well they fare forever,
By mighty dreams possessed,
Whose hearts have lain a moment
On that eternal breast.

THE RAINBIRD

I hear a rainbird singing
Far off. How fine and clear
His plaintive voice comes ringing
With rapture to the ear!

Over the misty wood-lots,
Across the first spring heat,
Comes the enchanted cadence,
So clear, so solemn-sweet.

How often I have hearkened
To that high pealing strain

Across wild cedar barrens,
Under the soft gray rain!

How often I have wondered,
And longed in vain to know
The source of that enchantment,
That touch of human woe!

O brother, who first taught thee
To haunt the teeming spring
With that sad mortal wisdom
Which only age can bring?

LAMENT

When you hear the white-throat pealing
From a tree-top far away,
And the hills are touched with purple
At the borders of the day;

When the redwing sounds his whistle
At the coming on of spring,
And the joyous April pipers
Make the alder marshes ring;

When the wild new breath of being
Whispers to the World once more,
And before the shrine of beauty
Every spirit must adore;

When long thoughts come back with twilight,
And a tender deepened mood
Shows the eyes of the beloved
Like hepaticas in the wood;

Ah, remember, when to nothing
Save to love your heart gives heed,
And spring takes you to her bosom,—
So it was with Golden Weed!

THRENODY FOR A POET

Not in the ancient abbey,
Nor in the city ground,

Not in the lonely mountains,
Nor in the blue profound,
Lay him to rest when his time is come
And the smiling mortal lips are dumb;

But here in the decent quiet
Under the whispering pines,
Where the dogwood breaks in blossom
And the peaceful sunlight shines,
Where wild birds sing and ferns unfold,
When spring comes back in her green and gold.

And when that mortal likeness
Has been dissolved by fire,
Say not above the ashes,
"Here ends a man's desire."
For every year when the bluebirds sing,
He shall be part of the lyric spring.

Then dreamful-hearted lovers
Shall hear in wind and rain
The cadence of his music,
The rhythm of his refrain,
For he was a blade of the April sod
That bowed and blew with the whisper of God.

UNDER THE APRIL MOON

Oh, well the world is dreaming
Under the April moon,
Her soul in love with beauty,
Her senses all a-swoon!

Pure hangs the silver crescent
Above the twilight wood,
And pure the silver music
Wakes from the marshy flood.

O Earth, with all thy transport,
How comes it life should seem
A shadow in the moonlight,
A murmur in a dream?

SPRING NIGHT

In the wondrous star-sown night,
In the first sweet warmth of spring,
I lie awake and listen
To hear the glad earth sing.

I hear the brook in the wood
Murmuring, as it goes,
The song of the happy journey
Only the wise heart knows.

I hear the trilling note
Of the tree-frog under the hill,
And the clear and watery treble
Of his brother, silvery shrill.

And then I wander away
Through the mighty forest of Sleep,
To follow the fairy music
To the shore of an endless deep.

IN EARLY MAY

O my dear, the world to-day
Is more lovely than a dream!
Magic hints from far away
Haunt the woodland, and the stream
Murmurs in his rocky bed
Things that never can be said.

Starry dogwood is in flower,
Gleaming through the mystic woods.
It is beauty's perfect hour
In the wild spring solitudes.
Now the orchards in full blow
Shed their petals white as snow.

All the air is honey-sweet
With the lilacs white and red,
Where the blossoming branches meet
In an arbor overhead.
And the laden cherry trees
Murmur with the hum of bees.

All the earth is fairy green,
And the sunlight filmy gold,

Full of ecstasies unseen,
Full of mysteries untold.
Who would not be out-of-door,
Now the spring is here once more!

FIREFLIES

The fireflies across the dusk
Are flashing signals through the gloom—
Courageous messengers of light
That dare immensities of doom.

About the seeding meadow-grass,
Like busy watchmen in the street,
They come and go, they turn and pass,
Lighting the way for Beauty's feet.

Or up they float on viewless wings
To twinkle high among the trees,
And rival with soft glimmerings
The shining of the Pleiades.

The stars that wheel above the hill
Are not more wonderful to see,
Nor the great tasks that they fulfil
More needed in eternity.

THE GARDEN OF DREAMS

My heart is a garden of dreams
Where you walk when day is done,
Fair as the royal flowers,
Calm as the lingering sun.

Never a drouth comes there,
Nor any frost that mars,
Only the wind of love
Under the early stars,—

The living breath that moves
Whispering to and fro,
Like the voice of God in the dusk
Of the garden long ago.

GARDEN SHADOWS

When the dawn winds whisper
To the standing corn,
And the rose of morning
From the dark is born,
All my shadowy garden
Seems to grow aware
Of a fragrant presence,
Half expected there.

In the golden shimmer
Of the burning noon,
When the birds are silent
And the poppies swoon,
Once more I behold her
Smile and turn her face,
With its infinite regard,
Its immortal grace.

When the twilight silvers
Every nodding flower,
And the new moon hallows
The first evening hour,
Is it not her footfall
Down the garden walks,
Where the drowsy blossoms
Slumber on their stalks?

In the starry quiet,
When the soul is free,
And a vernal message
Stirs the lilac tree,
Surely I have felt her
Pass and brush my cheek,
With the eloquence of love
That does not need to speak!

GARDEN MAGIC

Within my stone-walled garden
(I see her standing now,
Uplifted in the twilight,
With glory on her brow!)

I love to walk at evening
And watch, when winds are low,
The new moon in the tree-tops,
Because she loved it so!

And there entranced I listen,
While flowers and winds confer,
And all their conversation
Is redolent of her.

I love the trees that guard it,
Upstanding and serene,
So noble, so undaunted,
Because that was her mien.

I love the brook that bounds it,
Because its silver voice
Is like her bubbling laughter
That made the world rejoice.

I love the golden jonquils,
Because she used to say,
If Soul could choose a color
It would be clothed as they.

I love the blue-gray iris,
Because her eyes were blue,
Sea-deep and heaven-tender
In meaning and in hue.

I love the small wild roses,
Because she used to stand
Adoringly above them
And bless them with her hand.

These were her boon companions,
But more than all the rest
I love the April lilac,
Because she loved it best.

Soul of undying rapture!
How love's enchantment clings,
With sorcery and fragrance,
About familiar things!

NEW ENGLAND JUNE

These things I remember
Of New England June,
Like a vivid day-dream
In the azure noon,
While one haunting figure
Strays through every scene,
Like the soul of beauty
Through her lost demesne.

Gardens full of roses
And peonies a-blow
In the dewy morning,
Row on stately row,
Spreading their gay patterns,
Crimson, pied and cream,
Like some gorgeous fresco
Or an Eastern dream.

Nets of waving sunlight
Falling through the trees;
Fields of gold-white daisies
Rippling in the breeze;
Lazy lifting groundswells,
Breaking green as jade
On the lilac beaches,
Where the shore-birds wade.

Orchards full of blossom,
Where the bob-white calls
And the honeysuckle
Climbs the old gray walls;
Groves of silver birches,
Beds of roadside fern,
In the stone-fenced pasture
At the river's turn.

Out of every picture
Still she comes to me
With the morning freshness
Of the summer sea, —
A glory in her bearing,
A sea-light in her eyes,
As if she could not forget
The spell of Paradise.

Thrushes in the deep woods,

With their golden themes,
Fluting like the choirs
At the birth of dreams.
Fireflies in the meadows
At the gate of Night,
With their fairy lanterns
Twinkling soft and bright.

Ah, not in the roses,
Nor the azure noon,
Nor the thrushes' music,
Lies the soul of June.
It is something finer,
More unfading far,
Than the primrose evening
And the silver star;

Something of the rapture
My beloved had,
When she made the morning
Radiant and glad,—
Something of her gracious
Ecstasy of mien,
That still haunts the twilight,
Loving though unseen.

When the ghostly moonlight
Walks my garden ground,
Like a leisurely patrol
On his nightly round,
These things I remember
Of the long ago,
While the slumbrous roses
Neither care nor know.

ROADSIDE FLOWERS

We are the roadside flowers,
Straying from garden grounds, —
Lovers of idle hours,
Breakers of ordered bounds.

If only the earth will feed us,
If only the wind be kind,
We blossom for those who need us,
The stragglers left behind.

And lo, the Lord of the Garden,
He makes his sun to rise,
And his rain to fall like pardon
On our dusty paradise.

On us he has laid the duty, —
The task of the wandering breed,—
To better the world with beauty,
Wherever the way may lead.

Who shall inquire of the season,
Or question the wind where it blows?
We blossom and ask no reason.
The Lord of the Garden knows.

THE GARDEN OF SAINT ROSE

This is a holy refuge,
The garden of Saint Rose,
A fragrant altar to that peace
The world no longer knows.

Below a solemn hillside,
Within the folding shade
Of overhanging beech and pine
Its walls and walks are laid.

Cool through the heat of summer,
Still as a sacred grove,
It has the rapt unworldly air
Of mystery and love.

All day before its outlook
The mist-blue mountains loom,
And in its trees at tranquil dusk
The early stars will bloom.

Down its enchanted borders
Glad ranks of color stand,
Like hosts of silent seraphim
Awaiting love's command.

Lovely in adoration
They wait in patient line,
Snow-white and purple and deep gold

About the rose-gold shrine.

And there they guard the silence,
While still from her recess
Through sun and shade Saint Rose looks down
In mellow loveliness.

She seems to say, "O stranger,
Behold how loving care
That gives its life for beauty's sake,
Makes everything more fair!

"Then praise the Lord of gardens
For tree and flower and vine,
And bless all gardeners who have wrought
A resting place like mine!"

SONGS OF THE GRASS

I

ON THE DUNES

Here all night on the dunes
In the rocking wind we sleep;
Watched by the sentry stars,
Lulled by the drone of the deep.

Till hark, in the chill of the dawn
A field lark wakes and cries,
And over the floor of the sea
We watch the round sun rise.

The world is washed once more
In a tide of purple and gold,
And the heart of the land is filled
With desires and dreams untold.

II

LORD OF MORNING

Lord of morning, light of day,
Sacred color-kindling sun,
We salute thee in the way, —

Pilgrims robed in rose and dun.

For thou art a pilgrim too,,
Overlord of all our band.
In thy fervor we renew
Qests we do not understand.

At thy summons we arise,
At thy touch put glory on,
And with glad unanxious eyes
Take the journey thou hast gone.

III

THE TRAVELLER

Before the night-blue fades
And the stars are quite gone,
I lift my head
At the noiseless tread
Of the angel of dawn.

I hear no word, yet my heart
Is beating apace;
Then in glory all still
On the eastern hill
I behold his face.

All day through the world he goes,
Making glad, setting free;
Then his day's work done,
On the galleon sun
He sinks in the sea.

THE WEED'S COUNSEL

Said a traveller by the way
Pausing, "What hast thou to say,
Flower by the dusty road,
That would ease a mortal's load?"

Traveller, hearken unto me!
I will tell thee how to see
Beauties in the earth and sky
Hidden from the careless eye.

I will tell thee how to hear
Nature's music wild and clear,—
Songs of midday and of dark
Such as many never mark,
Lyrics of creation sung
Ever since the world was young.

And thereafter thou shalt know
Neither weariness nor woe.

Thou shalt see the dawn unfold
Artistries of rose and gold,
And the sunbeams on the sea
Dancing with the wind for glee.
The red lilies of the moors
Shall be torches on the floors,
Where the field-lark lifts his cry
To rejoice the passer-by,
In a wide world rimmed with blue
Lovely as when time was new.

And thereafter thou shalt fare
Light of foot and free from care.

I will teach thee how to find
Lost enchantments of the mind
All about thee, never guessed
By indifferent unrest.
Thy distracted thought shall learn
Patience from the roadside fern,
And a sweet philosophy
From the flowering locust tree, —
While thy heart shall not disdain
The consolation of the rain.

Not an acre but shall give
Of its strength to help thee live.

With the many-wintered sun
Shall thy hardy course be run.
And the bright new moon shall be
A lamp to thy felicity.
When green-mantled spring shall come
Past thy door with flute and drum,
And when over wood and swamp
Autumn trails her scarlet pomp,
No misgiving shalt thou know,
Passing glad to rise and go.

So thy days shall be unrolled
Like a wondrous cloth of gold.

When gray twilight with her star
Makes a heaven that is not far,
Touched with shadows and with dreams,
Thou shalt hear the woodland streams
Singing through the starry night
Holy anthems of delight.
So the ecstasy of earth
Shall refresh thee as at birth,
And thou shalt arise each morn
Radiant with a soul reborn.

And this wisdom of a day
None shall ever take away.

What the secret, what the clew
The wayfarer must pursue?
Only one thing he must have
Who would share these transports brave.
Love within his heart must dwell
Like a bubbling roadside well,
For a spring to quicken thought,
Else my counsel comes to naught.
For without that quickening trust
We are less than roadside dust.

This, O traveller, is my creed, —
All the wisdom of the weed!

Then the traveller set his pack
Once more on his dusty back,
And trudged on for many a mile
Fronting fortune with a smile.

LOCKERBIE STREET

FOR THE BIRTHDAY OF JAMES WHITCOMB RILEY, OCTOBER 7, 1914

Lockerbie Street is a little street,
Just one block long;
But the days go there with a magical air,
The whole year long.
The sun in his journey across the sky
Slows his car as he passes by;

The sighing wind and the grieving rain
Change their tune and cease to complain;
And the birds have a wonderful call that seems
Like a street-cry out of the land of dreams;
For there the real and the make-believe meet.
Time does not hurry in Lockerbie Street.

Lockerbie Street is a little street,
Only one block long;
But the moonlight there is strange and fair
All the year long,
As ever it was in old romance,
When fairies would sing and fauns would dance,
Proving this earth is subject still
To a blithesome wonder-working Will,
Spreading beauty over the land,
That every beholder may understand
How glory shines round the Mercy-seat.
That is the gospel of Lockerbie Street.

Lockerbie Street is a little street,
Only one block long,
A little apart, yet near the heart
Of the city's throng.
If you are a stranger looking to find
Respite and cheer for soul and mind,
And have lost your way, and would inquire
For a street that will lead to Heart's Desire,—
To a place where the spirit is never old,
And gladness and love are worth more than gold, —
Ask the first boy or girl you meet!
Everyone knows where is Lockerbie Street.

Lockerbie Street is a little street,
Only one block long;
But never a street in all the world,
In story or song,
Is better beloved by old and young;
For there a poet has lived and sung,
Wise as an angel, glad as a bird,
Fearless and fond in every word,
Many a year. And if you would know
The secret of joy and the cure of woe,—
How to be gentle and brave and sweet,—
Ask your way to Lockerbie Street.

A PORTRAIT

A. M. M.

Behold her sitting in the sun
This lovely April morn,
As eager with the breath of life
As daffodils new-born!
A priestess of the toiling earth,
Yet kindred to the spheres,
A touch of the eternal spring
Is over all her years.

No fashion frets her dignity,
Untrammeled, debonair;
A fold of lace about her throat
Falls from her whitening hair.
A seraph visiting the earth
Might wear that fearless guise,
The heartening regard of such
All-comprehending eyes.

How comes she by preëminence,
Desired, beloved, revered?
Heroic living gained those heights
Through ills she never feared.
A spirit kindly as the dew
And daring as a flame,
With a distinguished, reckless wit
No eighty years could tame.

A mother of the Spartan strain,
She held self-rule and sway,
And single-handed braved the world
And bore the prize away.
No task too humble for her skill,
No worthy way too long;
She filled her work with ecstasy
And crowned it with a song.

The treasures she most dearly prized
Were of the rarest kind —
A gentle fortitude of soul
And honesty of mind.
To feed, to clothe, to teach, to cheer,
To guard and guide and save —
These were her fine accomplishments,
To these her best she gave.

With ringing word and instant cure
She draws from far and near
The gay, the witty, the forlorn,
Priest, artist, beggar, seer.
Unhesitant and sure they come,
Hearing the human call,
As of a mighty motherhood
That understands them all.

Ungrudging, without grief, she lives
Each charged potential hour,
Holding her loftiness of aim
With agelessness of power.
Immortal friendship, great with years!
She shames the faltering,
And heartens every struggling hope,
Like hyacinths in spring!

A REMEMBRANCE

Here in lovely New England
When summer is come, a sea-turn
Flutters a page of remembrance
In the volume of long ago.

Soft is the wind over Grand Pré
Stirring the heads of the grasses,
Sweet is the breath of the orchards
White with their apple-blow.

There at their infinite business
Of measuring time forever,
Murmuring songs of the sea,
The great tides come and go.

Over the dikes and the uplands
Wander the great cloud shadows,
Strange as the passing of sorrow,
Beautiful, solemn, and slow.

For, spreading her old enchantment
Of tender ineffable wonder,
Summer is there in the Northland!
How should my heart not know?

OFF MONOMOY

Have you sailed Nantucket Sound
By lightship, buoy, and bell,
And lain becalmed at noon
On an oily summer swell?

Lazily drooped the sail,
Moveless the pennant hung,
Sagging over the rail
Idle the main boom swung;

The sea, one mirror of shine
A single breath would destroy,
Save for the far low line
Of treacherous Monomoy.

Yet eastward there toward Spain,
What castled cities rise
From the Atlantic plain,
To our enchanted eyes!

Turret and spire and roof
Looming out of the sea,
Where the prosy chart gives proof
No cape nor isle can be!

Can a vision shine so clear
Wherein no substance dwells?
One almost harks to hear
The sound of the city's bells.

And yet no pealing notes
Within those belfries be,
Save echoes from the throats
Of ship-bells lost at sea.

For none shall anchor there
Save those who long of yore,
When tide and wind were fair,
Sailed and came back no more.

And none shall climb the stairs
Within those ghostly towers,
Save those for whom sad prayers
Went up through fateful hours.

O image of the world,
O mirage of the sea,
Cloud-built and foam-impearled,
What sorcery fashioned thee?

What architect of dream,
What painter of desire,
Conceived that fairy scheme
Touched with fantastic fire?

Even so our city of hope
We mortal dreamers rear
Upon the perilous slope
Above the deep of fear;

Leaving half-known the good
Our kindly earth bestows,
For the feigned beatitude
Of a future no man knows.

Lord of the summer sea,
Whose tides are in thy hand,
Into immensity
The vision at thy command

Fades now, and leaves no sign, —
No light nor bell nor buoy, —
Only the faint low line
Of dangerous Monomoy.

THE WORLD VOICE

I heard the summer sea
Murmuring to the shore
Some endless story of a wrong
The whole world must deplore.

I heard the mountain wind
Conversing with the trees
Of an old sorrow of the hills,
Mysterious as the sea's.

And all that haunted day
It seemed that I could hear
The echo of an ancient speech

Ring in my listening ear.

And then it came to me,
That all that I had heard
Was my own heart in the sea's voice
And the wind's lonely word.

PHI BETA KAPPA POEM

HARVARD, 1914

Sir, friends, and scholars, we are here to serve
A high occasion. Our New England wears
All her unrivalled beauty as of old;
And June, with scent of bayberry and rose
And song of orioles— as she only comes
By Massachusetts Bay —is here once more,
Companioning our fête of fellowship.

The open trails, South, West, and North, lead back
From populous cities or from lonely plains,
Ranch, pulpit, office, factory, desk, or mill,
To this fair tribunal of ambitious youth,
The shadowy town beside the placid Charles,
Where Harvard waits us through the passing years,
Conserving and administering still
Her savor for the gladdening of the race.

Yearly, of all the sons she has sent forth,
And men her admiration would adopt,
She summons whom she will back to her side
As if to ask, "How fares my cause of truth
In the great world beyond these studious walls?"
Here, from their store of life experience,
They must make answer as grace is given them,
And their plain creed, in verity, declare.
Among the many, there is sometimes called
One who, like Arnold's scholar gypsy poor,
Is but a seeker on the dusky way,
"Still waiting for the spark from heaven to fall."

He must bethink him first of other days,
And that old scholar of the seraphic smile,
As we recall him in this very place
With all the sweetest culture of his age,
His gentle courtesy and friendliness,

A chivalry of soul now strangely rare,
And that ironic wit which made him, too,
The unflinching critic and most dreaded foe
Of all things mean, unlovely, and untrue.
What Mr. Norton said, with that slow smile,
Has put the fear of God in many a heart,
Even while his hand encouraged eager youth.

From such enheartening who would not dare speak—
Seeing no truth can be too small to serve,
And no word worthless that is born of love?
Within the noisy workshop of the world,
Where still the strife is upward out of gloom,
Men doubt the value of high teaching —cry,
"What use is learning? Man must have his will!
The élan of life alone is paramount!
Away with old traditions! We are free!"
So folly mocks at truth in Freedom's name.
Pale Anarchy leads on, with furious shriek,
Her envious horde of reckless malcontents
And mad destroyers of the Commonwealth,
While Privilege with indifference grows corrupt,
Till the Republic stands in jeopardy
From following false idols and ideals,
Though sane men cry for honesty once more,
Order and duty and self-sacrifice.

Our world and all it holds of good for us
Our fathers and unselfish mothers made,
With noble passion and enduring toil,
Strenuous, frugal, reverent, and elate,
Caring above all else to guard and save
The ampler life of the intelligence
And the fine honor of a scrupulous code —
Ideals of manhood touched with the divine.

For this they founded these great schools we serve,
Harvard, Columbia, Princeton, Dartmouth, Yale,
Amherst and Williams, trusting to our hands
The heritage of all they held most high,
Possessions of the spirit and the mind,
Investments in the provinces of joy.
Vast provinces are these! And fortunate they
Who at their will may go adventuring there,
Exploring all the boundaries of Truth,
Learning the roads that run through Beauty's realm,
Sighting the pinnacles where Good meets God,
Encompassed by the eternal unknown sea!

Even for a little to o'erlook those lands,
The kingdoms of Religion, Science, Art,
Is to be made forever happier
With blameless memories that shall bring content
And inspiration for all after days.
And fortunate they whom destiny allows
To rest within those provinces and serve
The dominion of ideals all their lives.
For whoso will, putting dull greed aside,
And holding fond allegiance to the best,
May dwell there and find fortitude and joy.

In the free fellowship of kindred minds,
One band of scholar gypsies I have known,
Whose purpose all unworldly was to find
An answer to the riddle of the Earth —
A key that should unlock the book of life
And secrets of its sorceries reveal.

This, they discovered, had long since been found
And laid aside forgotten and unused.
Our dark young poet who from Dartmouth came
Was told the secret by his gypsy bride,
Who had it from a master over seas,
And he it was first hinted to the band
The magic of that universal lore,
Before the great Mysteriarch summoned him.
It was the doctrine of the threefold life,
The beginning of the end of all their doubt.

In that Victorian age it has become
So much the fashion now to half despise,
Within the shadow of Cathedral walls
They had been schooled, and heard the mellow chimes
For Lenten litanies and daily prayers,
With a mild, eloquent, beloved voice
Exhorting to all virtue and that peace
Surpassing understanding —casting there
That "last enchantment of the Middle Age,"
The spell of Oxford and her ritual.

So duteous youth was trained, until there grew
Restive outreaching in men's thought to find
Some certitude beyond the dusk of faith.
They cried on mysticism to be gone,
Mazed in the shadowy princedom of the soul.

Then as old creeds fell round them into dust,
They reached through science to belief in law,
Made reason paramount in man, and guessed
At reigning mind within the universe.
Piecing the fragments of a fair design
With reverent patience and courageous skill,
They saw the world from chaos step by step,
Under far-seeing guidance and restraint,
Emerge to order and to symmetry,
As logical and sure as music's own.

With Spencer, Darwin, Tyndall, and the rest,
Our band saw roads of knowledge open wide
Through the uncharted province of the truth,
As on they fared through that unfolding world.

Yet there they found no rest-house for the heart,
No wells sufficient for the spirit's thirst,
No shade nor glory for the senses starved. . . .
Turning— they fled by moonlit trails to seek
The magic principality of Art,
Where loveliness, not learning, rules supreme.
They stood intoxicated with delight before
The poised unanxious splendor of the Greek;
They mused upon the Gothic minsters gray,
Where mystic spirit took on mighty form,
Until their prayers to lovely churches turned —
(Like a remembrance of the Middle Age
They rose where Ralph or Bertram dreamed in stone);
Entranced they trod a painters' paradise,
Where color wasted by the Scituate shore
Between the changing marshes and the sea;
They heard the golden voice of poesie
Lulling the senses with its last caress
In Tennysonion accents pure and fine;
And all their laurels were for Beauty's brow,
Though toiling Reason went ungarlanded.

Then poisonous weeds of artifice sprang up,
Defiling Nature at her sacred source;
And there the questing World-soul could not stay,
Onward must journey with the changing time,
To come to this uncouth rebellious age,
Where not an ancient creed nor courtesy
Is underided, and each demagogue
Cries some new nostrum for the cure of ills.
To-day the unreasoning iconoclast
Would scoff at science and abolish art,

To let untutored impulse rule the world.

Let learning perish, and the race returns
To that first anarchy from which we came,
When spirit moved upon the deep and laid
The primal chaos under cosmic law.

And even now, in all our wilful might,
The satiated being cannot bide,
But to that austere country turns again,
The little province of the saints of God,
Where lofty peaks rise upward to the stars
From the gray twilight of Gethsemane,
And spirit dares to climb with wounded feet
Where justice, peace, and loving kindness are.
What says the lore of human power we hold
Through all these striving and tumultuous days?
"Why not accept each several bloom of good,
Without discarding good already gained,
As one might weed a garden overgrown —
Save the new shoots, yet not destroy the old?
Only the fool would root up his whole patch
Of fragrant flowers, to plant the newer seed."

Ah, softly, brothers! Have we not the key,
Whose first fine luminous use Plotinus gave,
Teaching that ecstasy must lead the man?
Three things, we see, men in this life require,
(As they are needed in the universe):
First of all spirit, energy, or love,
The soul and mainspring of created things;
Next wisdom, knowledge, culture, discipline,
To guide impetuous spirit to its goal;
And lastly strength, the sound apt instrument,
Adjusted and controlled to lawful needs.

The next world-teacher must be one whose word
Shall reaffirm the primacy of soul,
Hold scholarship in her high guiding place,
And recognize the body's equal right
To culture such as it has never known,
In power and beauty serving soul and mind.

Inheritors of this divine ideal,
With courage to be fine as well as strong,
Shall know what common manhood may become,
Regain the gladness of the sons of morn,
The radiance of immortality.

Out of heroic wanderings of the past,
And all the wayward gropings of our time,
Unswerved by doubt, unconquered by despair,
The messengers of such a hope must go;
As one who hears far off before the dawn,
On some lone trail among the darkling hills,
The hermit thrushes in the paling dusk,
And at the omen lifts his eyes to see
Above him, with its silent shafts of light,
The sunrise kindling all the peaks with fire.

A MOUNTAIN GATEWAY

I know a vale where I would go one day,
When June comes back and all the world once more
Is glad with summer. Deep in shade it lies
A mighty cleft between the bosoming hills,
A cool dim gateway to the mountains' heart.

On either side the wooded slopes come down,
Hemlock and beech and chestnut. Here and there
Through the deep forest laurel spreads and gleams,
Pink-white as Daphne in her loveliness.
Among the sunlit shadows I can see
That still perfection from the world withdrawn,
As if the wood-gods had arrested there
Immortal beauty in her breathless flight.

The road winds in from the broad river-lands,
Luring the happy traveller turn by turn
Up to the lofty mountains of the sky.
And as he marches with uplifted face,
Far overhead against the arching blue
Gray ledges overhang from dizzy heights,
Scarred by a thousand winters and untamed.

And where the road runs in the valley's foot,
Through the dark woods a mountain stream comes down,
Singing and dancing all its youth away
Among the boulders and the shallow runs,
Where sunbeams pierce and mossy tree trunks hang
Drenched all day long with murmuring sound and spray.

There light of heart and footfree, I would go
Up to my home among the lasting hills.

Nearing the day's end, I would leave the road,
Turn to the left and take the steeper trail
That climbs among the hemlocks, and at last
In my own cabin doorway sit me down,

Companioned in that leafy solitude
By the wood ghosts of twilight and of peace,
While evening passes to absolve the day
And leave the tranquil mountains to the stars.

And in that sweet seclusion I should hear,
Among the cool-leafed beeches in the dusk,
The calm-voiced thrushes at their twilight hymn.
So undistraught, so rapturous, so pure,
They well might be, in wisdom and in joy,
The seraphs singing at the birth of time
The unworn ritual of eternal things.

THE HOMESTEAD

Here we came when love was young.
Now that love is old,
Shall we leave the floor unswept
And the hearth acold?

Here the hill-wind in the dusk,
Wandering to and fro,
Moves the moonflowers, like a ghost
Of the long ago.

Here from every doorway looks
A remembered face,
Every sill and panel wears
A familiar grace.

Let the windows smile again
To the morning light,
And the door stand open wide
When the moon is bright.

Let the breeze of twilight blow
Through the silent hall,
And the dreaming rafters hear
How the thrushes call.

Oh, be merciful and fond

To the house that gave
All its best to shelter love,
Built when love was brave!

Here we came when love was young.
Now that love is old,
Never let its day be lone,
Nor its heart acold!

AT SUNRISE

Now the stars have faded
In the purple chill,
Lo, the sun is kindling
On the eastern hill.

Tree by tree the forest
Takes the golden tinge,
As the shafts of glory
Pierce the summit's fringe.

Rock by rock the ledges
Take the rosy sheen,
As the tide of splendor
Floods the dark ravine.

Like a shining angel
At my cabin door,
Shod with hope and silence,
Day is come once more.

Then, as if in sorrow
That you are not here,
All his magic beauties
Gray and disappear.

AT TWILIGHT

Now the fire is lighted
On the chimney stone,
Day goes down the valley,
I am left alone.

Now the misty purple

Floods the darkened vale,
And the stars come out
On the twilight trail.

The mountain river murmurs
In his rocky bed,
And the stealthy shadows
Fill the house with dread.

Then I hear your laughter
At the open door, —
Brightly burns the fire,
I need fear no more.

NIGHT LYRIC

On the world's far edges
Faint and blue,
Where the rocky ledges
Stand in view,

Fades the rosy tender
Evening light;
Then in starry splendor
Comes the night.

So a stormy lifetime
Comes to close,
Spirit's mortal strife-time
Finds repose.

Faith and toil and vision
Crowned at last,
Failure and derision
Overpast,—

All the daylight splendor
Far above,
Calm and sure and tender
Comes thy love.

WEATHER OF THE SOUL

There is a world of being

We range from pole to pole,
Through seasons of the spirit
And weather of the soul.

It has its new-born Aprils,
With gladness in the air,
Its golden Junes of rapture,
Its winters of despair.

And in its tranquil autumns
We halt to re-enforce
Our tattered scarlet pennons
With valor and resource.

From undiscovered regions
Only the angels know,
Great winds of aspiration
Perpetually blow,

To free the sap of impulse
From torpor of distrust,
And into flowers of joyance
Quicken the sentient dust.

From nowhere of a sudden
Loom sudden clouds of fault,
With thunders of oppression
And lightnings of revolt.

With hush of apprehension
And quaking of the heart,
There breed the storms of anger,
And floods of sorrow start.

And there shall fall,—how gently!—
To make them fertile yet,
The rain of absolution
On acres of regret.

Till snows of mercy cover
The dream that shall come true,
When time makes all things wondrous,
And life makes all things new.

WOODLAND RAIN

Shining, shining children
Of the summer rain,
Racing down the valley,
Sweeping o'er the plain!

Rushing through the forest,
Pelting on the leaves,
Drenching down the meadow
With its standing sheaves;

Robed in royal silver,
Girt with jewels gay,
With a gust of gladness
You pass upon your way.

Fresh, ah, fresh behind you,
Sunlit and impearled,
As it was in Eden,
Lies the lovely world!

THE TENT OF NOON

Behold, now, where the pageant of high June
Halts in the glowing noon!
The trailing shadows rest on plain and hill;
The bannered hosts are still,
While over forest crown and mountain head
The azure tent is spread.

The song is hushed in every woodland throat;
Moveless the lilies float;
Even the ancient ever-murmuring sea
Sighs only fitfully;
The cattle drowse in the field-corner's shade;
Peace on the world is laid.

It is the hour when Nature's caravan,
That bears the pilgrim Man
Across the desert of uncharted time
To his far hope sublime,
Rests in the green oasis of the year,
As if the end drew near.

Ah, traveller, hast thou naught of thanks or praise
For these fleet halcyon days? —
No courage to uplift thee from despair

Born with the breath of prayer?
Then turn thee to the lilied field once more!
God stands in his tent door.

SUMMER STORM

The hilltop trees are bowing
Under the coming of storm.
The low gray clouds are trailing
Like squadrons that sweep and form,
With their ammunition of rain.

Then the trumpeter wind gives signal
To unlimber the viewless guns;
The cattle huddle together;
Indoors the farmer runs;
And the first shot lashes the pane.

They charge through the quiet orchard;
One pear tree is snapped like a wand;
As they sweep from the shattered hillside,
Ruffling the blackened pond,
Ere the sun takes the field again.

DANCE OF THE SUNBEAMS

When morning is high o'er the hilltops
On river and stream and lake,
Wherever a young breeze whispers,
The sun-clad dancers wake.

One after one up-springing,
They flash from their dim retreat.
Merry as running laughter
Is the news of their twinkling feet.

Over the floors of azure
Wherever the wind-flaws run,
Sparkling, leaping, and racing,
Their antics scatter the sun.

As long as water ripples
And weather is clear and glad,
Day after day they are dancing,

Never a moment sad.

But when through the field of heaven
The wings of storm take flight,
At a touch of the flying shadows
They falter and slip from sight.

Until at the gray day's ending,
As the squadrons of cloud retire,
They pass in the triumph of sunset
With banners of crimson fire.

THE CAMPFIRE OF THE SUN

Lo, now, the journeying sun,
Another day's march done,
Kindles his campfire at the edge of night!
And in the twilight pale
Above his crimson trail,
The stars move out their cordons still and bright.

Now in the darkening hush
A solitary thrush
Sings on in silvery rapture to the deep;
While brooding on her best,
The wandering soul has rest,
And earth receives her sacred gift of sleep.

MOONRISE

AT the end of the road through the wood
I see the great moon rise.
The fields are flooded with shine,
And my soul with surmise.

What if that mystic orb
With her shadowy beams,
Should be the revealer at last
Of my darkest dreams!

What if this tender fire
In my heart's deep hold
Should be wiser than all the lore
Of the sages of old!

THE QUEEN OF NIGHT

Mortal, mortal, have you seen
In the scented summer night,
Great Astarte, clad in green
With a veil of mystic light,
Passing on her silent way,
Pale and lovelier than day?

Mortal, mortal, have you heard,
On an odorous summer eve,
Rumors of an unknown word
Bidding sorrow not to grieve,—
Echoes of a silver voice
Bidding every heart rejoice?

Mortal, when the slim new moon
Hangs above the western hill,
When the year comes round to June
And the leafy world is still,
Then, enraptured, you shall hear
Secrets for a poet's ear.

Mortal, mortal, come with me,
When the moon is rising large,
Through the wood or from the sea,
Or by some lone river marge.
There, entranced, you shall behold
Beauty's self, that grows not old.

SUMMER STREAMS

All day long beneath the sun
Shining through the fields they run,

Singing in a cadence known
To the seraphs round the throne.

And the traveller drawing near
Through the meadow, halts to hear

Anthems of a natural joy
No disaster can destroy.

All night long from set of sun
Through the starry woods they run,

Singing through the purple dark
Songs to make a traveller hark.

All night long, when winds are low,
Underneath my window go

The immortal happy streams,
Making music through my dreams.

THE GOD OF THE WOOD

Here all the forces of the wood
As one converge,
To make the soul of solitude
Where all things merge.

The sun, the rain-wind, and the rain,
The visiting moon,
The hurrying cloud by peak and plain,
Each with its boon.

Here power attains perfection still
In mighty ease,
That the great earth may have her will
Of joy and peace.

And so through me, the mortal born
Of plasmic clay,
Immortal powers, kind, fierce, forlorn,
And glad, have sway.

Eternal passions, ardors fine,
And monstrous fears,
Rule and rebel, serene, malign,
Or loosed in tears;

Until at last they shall evolve
From griefs and joys
Some steady light, some firm resolve,
Some Godlike poise.

THE GIFT

I said to Life, "How comes it,
With all this wealth in store,
Of beauty, joy, and knowledge,
Thy cry is still for more?

"Count all the years of striving
To make thy burden less, —
The things designed and fashioned
To gladden thy success!

"The treasures sought and gathered
Thy lightest whim to please, —
The loot of all the ages,
The spoil of all the seas!

"Is there no end of labor,
No limit to thy need?
Must man go bowed forever
In bondage to thy greed?"

With tears of pride and passion
She answered, "God above!
I only wait the asking,
To spend it all for love!"

THE GIVERS OF LIFE

I.

Who called us forth out of darkness and gave us the gift of life,
Who set our hands to the toiling, our feet in the field of strife?

Darkly they mused, predestined to knowledge of viewless things,
Sowing the seed of wisdom, guarding the living springs.

Little they reckoned privation, hunger or hardship or cold,
If only the life might prosper, and the joy that grows not old.

With sorceries subtler than music, with knowledge older than speech,
Gentle as wind in the wheat-field, strong as the tide on the beach,

Out of their beauty and longing, out of their raptures and tears,
In patience and pride they bore us, to war with the warring years.

II.

Who looked on the world before them, and summoned and chose our sires,
Subduing the wayward impulse to the will of their deep desires?

Sovereigns of ultimate issues under the greater laws,
Theirs was the mystic mission of the eternal cause;

Confident, tender, courageous, leaving the low for the higher,
Lifting the feet of the nations out of the dust and the mire;

Luring civilization on to the fair and new,
Given God's bidding to follow, having God's business to do.

III.

Who strengthened our souls with courage, and taught us the ways of Earth?
Who gave us our patterns of beauty, our standards of flawless worth?

Mothers, unmilitant, lovely, moulding our manhood then,
Walked in their woman's glory, swaying the might of men.

They schooled us to service and honor, modest and clean and fair, —
The code of their worth of living, taught with the sanction of prayer.

They were our sharers of sorrow, they were our makers of joy,
Lighting the lamp of manhood in the heart of the lonely boy.

Haloed with love and with wonder, in sheltered ways they trod,
Seers of sublime divination, keeping the truce of God.

IV.

Who called us from youth and dreaming, and set ambition alight,
And made us fit for the contest, —men, by their tender rite?

Sweethearts above our merit, charming our strength and skill
To be the pride of their loving, to be the means of their will.

If we be the builders of beauty, if we be the masters of art,
Theirs were the gleaming ideals, theirs the uplift of the heart.

Truly they measure the lightness of trappings and ease and fame,
For the teeming desire of their yearning is ever and ever the same:

To crown their lovers with gladness, to clothe their sons with delight,
And see the men of their making lords in the best man's right.

Lavish of joy and labor, broken only by wrong,
These are the guardians of being, spirited, sentient and strong.

Theirs is the starry vision, theirs the inspiriting hope,
Since Night, the brooding enchantress, promised that day should ope.

V.

Lo, we have built and invented, reasoned, discovered and planned,
To rear us a palace of splendor, and make us a heaven by hand.

We are shaken with dark misgiving, as kingdoms rise and fall;
But the women who went to found them are never counted at all.

Versed in the soul's traditions, skilled in humanity's lore,
They wait for their crown of rapture, and weep for the sins of war.

And behold they turn from our triumphs, as it was in the first of days,
For a little heaven of ardor and a little heartening of praise.

These are the rulers of kingdoms beyond the domains of state,
Martyrs of all men's folly, over-rulers of fate.

These we will love and honor, these we will serve and defend,
Fulfilling the pride of nature, till nature shall have an end.

VI.

This is the code unwritten, this is the creed we hold,
Guarding the little and lonely, gladdening the helpless and old,—

Apart from the brunt of the battle our wondrous women shall bide,
For the sake of a tranquil wisdom and the need of a spirit's guide.

Come they into assembly, or keep they another door,
Our makers of life shall lighten the days as the years of yore.

The lure of their laughter shall lead us, the lilt of their words shall sway.
Though life and death should defeat us, their solace shall be our stay.

Veiled in mysterious beauty, vested in magical grace,
They have walked with angels at twilight and looked upon glory's face.

Life we will give for their safety, care for their fruitful ease,
Though we break at the toiling benches or go down in the smoky seas.

This is the gospel appointed to govern a world of men,
Till love has died, and the echoes have whispered the last Amen.

IN THE DAY OF BATTLE

In the day of battle,
In the night of dread,
Let one hymn be lifted,
Let one prayer be said.

Not for pride of conquest,
Not for vengeance wrought,
Nor for peace and safety
With dishonor bought!

Praise for faith in freedom,
Our fighting fathers' stay,
Born of dreams and daring,
Bred above dismay.

Prayer for cloudless vision,
And the valiant hand,
That the right may triumph
To the last demand.

PEACE

The sleeping tarn is dark
Below the wooded hill.
Save for its homing sounds,
The twilit world grows still.

And I am left to muse
In grave-eyed mystery,
And watch the stars come out
As sandalled dusk goes by.

And now the light is gone,
The drowsy murmurs cease,
And through the still unknown

I wonder whence comes peace.

Then softly falls the word
Of one beyond a name,
"Peace only comes to him
Who guards his life from shame, —

"Who gives his heart to love,
And holding truth for guide,
Girds him with fearless strength,
That freedom may abide."

TREES

In the Garden of Eden, planted by God,
There were goodly trees in the springing sod,—

Trees of beauty and height and grace,
To stand in splendor before His face.

Apple and hickory, ash and pear,
Oak and beech and the tulip rare,

The trembling aspen, the noble pine,
The sweeping elm by the river line;

Trees for the birds to build and sing,
And the lilac tree for a joy in spring;

Trees to turn at the frosty call
And carpet the ground for their Lord's footfall;

Trees for fruitage and fire and shade,
Trees for the cunning builder's trade;

Wood for the bow, the spear, and the flail,
The keel and the mast of the daring sail;

He made them of every grain and girth
For the use of man in the Garden of Earth.

Then lest the soul should not lift her eyes
From the gift to the Giver of Paradise,

On the crown of a hill, for all to see,
God planted a scarlet maple tree.

IN OCTOBER

Now come the rosy dogwoods,
The golden tulip-tree,
And the scarlet yellow maple,
To make a day for me.

The ash-trees on the ridges,
The alders in the swamp,
Put on their red and purple
To join the autumn pomp.

The woodbine hangs her crimson
Along the pasture wall,
And all the bannered sumacs
Have heard the frosty call.

Who then so dead to valor
As not to raise a cheer,
When all the woods are marching
In triumph of the year?

A FIRESIDE VISION

Once I walked the world enchanted
Through the scented woods of spring,
Hand in hand with Love, in rapture
Just to hear a bluebird sing.

Now the lonely winds of autumn
Moan about my gusty eaves,
As I sit beside the fire
Listening to the flying leaves.

As the dying embers settle
And the twilight falls apace,
Through the gloom I see a vision
Full of ardor, full of grace.

When the Architect of Beauty
Breathed the lyric soul in man,
Lo, the being that he fashioned
Was of such a mould and plan!

Bravely through the deepening shadows
Moves that figure half divine,
With its tenderness of bearing,
With its dignity of line.

Eyes more wonderful than evening.
With the new moon on the hill,
Mouth with traces of God's humor
In its corners lurking still.

Ah, she smiles, in recollection;
Lays a hand upon my brow;
Rests this head upon Love's bosom!
Surely it is April now!

THE BLUE HERON

I see the great blue heron
Rising among the reeds
And floating down the wind,
Like a gliding sail
With the set of the stream.

I hear the two-horse mower
Clacking among the hay,
In the heat of a July noon,
And the driver's voice
As he turns his team.

I see the meadow lilies
Flecked with their darker tan,
The elms, and the great white clouds;
And all the world
Is a passing dream.

A WINTER PIECE

Over the rim of a lacquered bowl,
Where a cold blue water-color stands
I see the wintry breakers roll
And heave their froth up the freezing sands.

Here in immunity safe and dull,

Soul treads her circuit of trivial things.
There soul's brother, a shining gull,
Dares the rough weather on dauntless wings.

THE GHOST-YARD OF THE GOLDENROD

When the first silent frost has trod
The ghost-yard of the goldenrod,

And laid the blight of his cold hand
Upon the warm autumnal land,

And all things wait the subtle change
That men call death, is it not strange

That I— without a care or need,
Who only am an idle weed —

Should wait unmoved, so frail, so bold,
The coming of the final cold!

BEFORE THE SNOW

Now soon, ah, very soon, I know
The trumpets of the north will blow,
And the great winds will come to bring
The pale wild riders of the snow.

Darkening the sun with level flight,
At arrowy speed, they will alight,
Unnumbered as the desert sands,
To bivouac on the edge of night.

Then I, within their somber ring,
Shall hear a voice that seems to sing,
Deep, deep within my tranquil heart,
The valiant prophecy of spring.

WINTER TWILIGHT

Along the wintry skyline,
Crowning the rocky crest,
Stands the bare screen of hardwood trees

Against the saffron west,—
Its gray and purple network
Of branching tracery
Outspread upon the lucent air,
Like weed within the sea.

The scarlet robe of autumn
Renounced and put away,
The mystic Earth is fairer still, —
A Puritan in gray.
The spirit of the winter,
How tender, how austere!
Yet all the ardor of the spring
And summer's dream are here.

Fear not, O timid lover,
The touch of frost and rime!
This is the virtue that sustained
The roses in their prime.
The anthem of the northwind
Shall hallow thy despair,
The benediction of the snow
Be answer to thy prayer.

And now the star of evening
That is the pilgrim's sign,
Is lighted in the primrose dusk, —
A lamp before a shrine.
Peace fills the mighty minster,
Tranquil and gray and old,
And all the chancel of the west
Is bright with paling gold.

A little wind goes sifting
Along the meadow floor,—
Like steps of lovely penitents
Who sighingly adore.
Then falls the twilight curtain,
And fades the eerie light,
And frost and silence turn the keys
In the great doors of night.

A CHRISTMAS EVE CHORAL

HALLELUJA!

What sound is this across the dark

While all the earth is sleeping? Hark!
Halleluja! Halleluja! Halleluja!

Why are thy tender eyes so bright,
Mary, Mary?
On the prophetic deep of night
Joseph, Joseph,
I see the borders of the light,
And in the day that is to be
An aureoled man-child I see,
Great love's son, Joseph.

Halleluja!
He hears not, but she hears afar,
The Minstrel Angel of the star.
Halleluja! Halleluja! Halleluja!

Why is thy gentle smile so deep,
Mary, Mary?
It is the secret I must keep,
Joseph, Joseph, —
The joy that will not let me sleep,
The glory of the coming days,
When all the world shall turn to praise
God's goodness, Joseph.

Halleluja!
Clear as the bird that brings the morn
She hears the heavenly music borne.
Halleluja! Halleluja! Halleluja!

Why is thy radiant face so calm,
Mary, Mary?
His strength is like a royal palm,
Joseph, Joseph;
His beauty like the victor's psalm,
He moves like morning o'er the lands
And there is healing in his hands
For sorrow, Joseph.

Halleluja!
Tender as dew-fall on the earth
She hears the choral of love's birth.
Halleluja! Halleluja! Halleluja!

What is the message come to thee,
Mary, Mary?
I hear like wind within the tree,

Joseph, Joseph,
Or like a far-off melody
His deathless voice proclaiming peace,
And bidding ruthless wrong to cease,
For love's sake, Joseph.

Halleluja!
Moving as rain-wind in the spring
She hears the angel chorus ring.
Halleluja! Halleluja! Halleluja!

Why are thy patient hands so still,
Mary, Mary?
I see the shadow on the hill,
Joseph, Joseph,
And wonder if it is God's will
That courage, service, and glad youth
Shall perish in the cause of truth
Forever, Joseph.

Halleluja!
Her heart in that celestial chime
Has heard the harmony of time.
Halleluja! Halleluja! Halleluja!

Why is thy voice so strange and far,
Mary, Mary?
I see the glory of the star,
Joseph, Joseph,
And in its light all things that are
Made glad and wise beyond the sway
Of death and darkness and dismay,
In God's time, Joseph.

Halleluja!
To every heart in love 't is given
To hear the ecstasy of heaven.
Halleluja! Halleluja! Halleluja!

THE SENDING OF THE MAGI

In a far Eastern country
It happened long of yore,
Where a lone and level sunrise
Flushes the desert floor,
That three kings sat together

And a spearman kept the door.

Gaspar, whose wealth was counted
By city and caravan;
With Melchior, the seer
Who read the starry plan;
And Balthasar, the blameless,
Who loved his fellow man.

There while they talked, a sudden
Strange rushing sound arose,
And as with startled faces
They thought upon their foes,
Three figures stood before them
In imperial repose.

One in flame-gold and one in blue
And one in scarlet clear,
With the almighty portent
Of sunrise they drew near!
And the kings made obeisance
With hand on breast, in fear.

"Arise," said they, "we bring you
Good tidings of great peace!
To-day a power is wakened
Whose working must increase,
Till fear and greed and malice
And violence shall cease."

The messengers were Michael,
By whom all things are wrought
To shape and hue; and Gabriel
Who is the lord of thought;
And Rafael without whose love
All toil must come to nought.

Then Rafael said to Balthasar,
"In a country west from here
A lord is born in lowliness,
In love without a peer.
Take grievances and gifts to him
And prove his kingship clear!

"By this sign ye shall know him;
Within his mother's arm
Among the sweet-breathed cattle
He slumbers without harm,

While wicked hearts are troubled
And tyrants take alarm."

And Gabriel said to Melchior,
"My comrade, I will send
My star to go before you,
That ye may comprehend
Where leads your mystic learning
In a humaner trend."

And Michael said to Gaspar,
"Thou royal builder, go
With tribute of thy riches!
Though time shall overthrow
Thy kingdom, no undoing
His gentle might shall know."

Then while the kings' hearts greatened
And all the chamber shone,
As when the hills at sundown
Take a new glory on
And the air thrills with purple,
Their visitors were gone.

Then straightway up rose Gaspar,
Melchior and Balthasar,
And passed out through the murmur
Of palace and bazar,
To make without misgiving
The journey of the Star.

CHRISTMAS SONG

Above the weary waiting world,
Asleep in chill despair,
There breaks a sound of joyous bells
Upon the frosted air.
And o'er the humblest rooftree, lo,
A star is dancing on the snow.

What makes the yellow star to dance
Upon the brink of night?
What makes the breaking dawn to glow
So magically bright,—
And all the earth to be renewed
With infinite beatitude?

The singing bells, the throbbing star,
The sunbeams on the snow,
And the awakening heart that leaps
New ecstasy to know, —
They all are dancing in the morn
Because a little child is born.

WINTER STREAMS

Now the little rivers go
Muffled safely under snow,

And the winding meadow streams
Murmur in their wintry dreams,

While a tinkling music wells
Faintly from their icy bells,

Telling how their hearts are bold
Though the very sun be cold.

Ah, but wait until the rain
Comes a-sighing once again,

Sweeping softly from the Sound
Over ridge and meadow ground!

Then the little streams will hear
April calling far and near,—

Slip their snowy bands and run
Sparkling in the welcome sun.

Bliss Carman - An Appreciation

How many Canadians—how many even among the few who seek to keep themselves informed of the best in contemporary literature, who are ever on the alert for the new voices—realise, or even suspect, that this Northern land of theirs has produced a poet of whom it may be affirmed with confidence and assurance that he is of the great succession of English poets? Yet such—strange and unbelievable though it may seem—is in very truth the case, that poet being (to give him his full name) William Bliss Carman. Canada has full right to be proud of her poets, a small body though they are; but not only does Mr. Carman stand high and clear above them all—his place (and time cannot but confirm and justify the assertion) is among those men whose poetry is the shining glory of that great English literature which is our common heritage.

If any should ask why, if what has been just said is so, there has been—as must be admitted—no general recognition of the fact in the poet's home land, I would answer that there are various and plausible, if not good, reasons for it.

First of all, the poet, as thousands more of our young men of ambition and confidence have done, went early to the United States, and until recently, except for rare and brief visits to his old home down by the sea, has never returned to Canada—though for all that, I am able to state, on his own authority, he is still a Canadian citizen. Then all his books have had their original publication in the United States, and while a few of them have subsequently carried the imprints of Canadian publishers, none of these can be said ever to have made any special effort to push their sale. Another reason for the fact above mentioned is that Mr. Carman has always scorned to advertise himself, while his work has never been the subject of the log-rolling and booming which the work of many another poet has had—to his ultimate loss. A further reason is that he follows a rule of his own in preparing his books for publication. Most poets publish a volume of their work as soon as, through their industry and perseverance, they have material enough on hand to make publication desirable in their eyes. Not so with Mr. Carman, however, his rule being not to publish until he has done sufficient work of a certain general character or key to make a volume. As a result, you cannot fully know or estimate his work by one book, or two books, or even half a dozen; you must possess or be familiar with every one of the score and more volumes which contain his output of poetry before you can realise how great and how many-sided is his genius.

It is a common remark on the part of those who respond readily to the vigorous work of Kipling, or Masefield, even our own Service, that Bliss Carman's poetry has no relation to or concern with ordinary, everyday life. One would suppose that most persons who cared for poetry at all turned to it as a relief from or counter to the burdens and vexations of the daily round; but in any event, the remark referred to seems to me to indicate either the most casual acquaintance with Mr. Carman's work, or a complete misunderstanding and misapprehension of the meaning of it. I grant that you will find little or nothing in it all to remind you of the grim realities and vexing social problems of this modern existence of ours; but to say or to suggest that these things do not exist for Mr. Carman is to say or to suggest something which is the reverse of true. The truth is, he is aware of them as only one with the sensitive organism of a poet can be; but he does not feel that he has a call or mission to remedy them, and still less to sing of them. He therefore leaves the immediate problems of the day to those who choose, or are led, to occupy themselves therewith, and turns resolutely away to dwell upon those things which for him possess infinitely greater importance.

"What are they?" one who knows Mr. Carman only as, say, a lyrist of spring or as a singer of the delights of vagabondia probably will ask in some wonder. Well, the things which concern him above all, I would answer, are first, and naturally, the beauty and wonder of this world of ours, and next the mystery of the earthly pilgrimage of the human soul out of eternity and back into it again.

The poems in the present volume—which, by the way, can boast the high honor of being the very first regular Canadian edition of his work—will be evidence ample and conclusive to every reader, I am sure, of the place which

The perennial enchanted

Lovely world and all its lore

occupy in the heart and soul of Bliss Carman, as well as of the magical power with which he is able to convey the deep and unfailing satisfaction and delight which they possess for him. They, however, represent his latest period (he has had three well-defined periods), comprising selections from three of his last published volumes: The Rough Rider, Echoes from Vagabondia, and April Airs, together with a number of new poems, and do not show, except here and there and by hints and flashes, how great is his preoccupation with the problem of man's existence—

—the hidden import
Of man's eternal plight.

This is manifest most in certain of his earlier books, for in these he turns and returns to the greatest of all the problems of man almost constantly, probing, with consummate and almost unrivalled use of the art of expression, for the secret which surely, he clearly feels, lies hidden somewhere, to be discovered if one could but pierce deeply enough. Pick up Behind the Arras, and as you turn over page after page you cannot but observe how incessantly the poet's mind—like the minds of his two great masters, Browning and Whitman—works at this problem. In "Behind the Arras," the title poem; "In the Wings," "The Crimson House," "The Lodger," "Beyond the Gamut," "The Juggler"—yes, in every poem in the book—he takes up and handles the strange thing we know as, or call, life, turning it now this way, now that, in an effort to find out its meaning and purpose. He comes but little nearer success in this than do most of the rest of men, of course; but the magical and ever-fresh beauty of his expression, the haunting melody of his lines, the variety of his images and figures and the depth and range of his thought, put his searchings and ponderings in a class by themselves.

Lengthy quotation from Mr. Carman's books is not permitted here, and I must guide myself accordingly, though with reluctance, because I believe that in a study such as this the subject should be allowed to speak for himself as much as possible. In "Behind the Arras" the poet describes the passage from life to death as

A cadence dying down unto its source
In music's course,

and goes on to speak of death as

—the broken rhythm of thought and man,
The sweep and span
Of memory and hope
About the orbit where they still must grope
For wider scope,

To be through thousand springs restored, renewed,
With love imbrued,
With increments of will
Made strong, perceiving unattainment still
From each new skill.

Now follow some verses from "Behind the Gamut," to my mind the poet's greatest single achievement;

As fine sand spread on a disc of silver,
At some chord which bids the motes combine,
Heeding the hidden and reverberant impulse,
Shifts and dances into curve and line,

The round earth, too, haply, like a dust-mote,
Was set whirling her assigned sure way,
Round this little orb of her ecliptic
To some harmony she must obey.

And what of man?

Linked to all his half-accomplished fellows,
Through unfrontiered provinces to range—
Man is but the morning dream of nature,
Roused to some wild cadence weird and strange.

Here, now, are some verses from "Pulvis et Umbra," which is to be found in Mr. Carman's first book, Low Tide on Grand Pré, and in which the poet addresses a moth which a storm has blown into his window:

For man walks the world with mourning
Down to death and leaves no trace,
With the dust upon his forehead,
And the shadow on his face.

Pillared dust and fleeing shadow
As the roadside wind goes by,
And the fourscore years that vanish
In the twinkling of an eye.

"Pillared dust and fleeing shadow." Where in all our English literature will one find the life history of man summed up more briefly and, at the same time, more beautifully, than in that wonderful line? Now follows a companion verse to those just quoted, taken from "Lord of My Heart's Elation," which stands in the forefront of From the Green Book of the Bards. It may be remarked here that while the poet recurs again and again to some favorite thought or idea, it is never in the same words. His expression is always new and fresh, showing how deep and true is his inspiration. Again it is man who is pictured:

A fleet and shadowy column
Of dust and mountain rain,
To walk the earth a moment
And be dissolved again.

But while Mr. Carman's speculations upon life's meaning and the mystery of the future cannot but appeal to the thoughtful-minded, it is as an interpreter of nature that he makes his widest appeal. Bliss Carman, I must say here, and emphatically, is no mere landscape-painter; he never, or scarcely ever, paints a picture of nature for its own sake. He goes beyond the outward aspect of things and interprets or translates for us with less keen senses as only a poet whose feeling for nature is of the deepest and profoundest, who has gone to her whole-heartedly and been taken close to her warm bosom, can do. Is this not evident from these verses from "The Great Return"—originally called "The Pagan's Prayer," and for some inscrutable reason to be found only in the limited Collected Poems, issued in two stately volumes in 1905.

When I have lifted up my heart to thee,
Thou hast ever hearkened and drawn near,
And bowed thy shining face close over me,
Till I could hear thee as the hill-flowers hear.

When I have cried to thee in lonely need,
Being but a child of thine bereft and wrung,
Then all the rivers in the hills gave heed;
And the great hill-winds in thy holy tongue—

That ancient incommunicable speech—
The April stars and autumn sunsets know—
Soothed me and calmed with solace beyond reach
Of human ken, mysterious and low.

Who can read or listen to those moving lines without feeling that Mr. Carman is in very truth a poet of nature—nay, Nature's own poet? But how could he be other when, in "The Breath of the Reed" (From the Green Book of the Bards), he makes the appeal?

Make me thy priest, O Mother,
And prophet of thy mood,
With all the forest wonder
Enraptured and imbued.

As becomes such a poet, and particularly a poet whose birth-month is April, Mr. Carman sings much of the early spring. Again and again he takes up his woodland pipe, and lo! Pan himself and all his train troop joyously before us. Yet the singer's notes for all his singing never become wearied or strident; his airs are ever new and fresh; his latest songs are no less spontaneous and winning than were his first, written how many years ago, while at the same time they have gained in beauty and melody. What heart will not stir to the vibrant music of his immortal "Spring Song," which was originally published in the first Songs from Vagabondia, and the opening verses of which follow?

Make me over, mother April,
When the sap begins to stir!
When thy flowery hand delivers
All the mountain-prisoned rivers,
And thy great heart beats and quivers
To revive the days that were,
Make me over, mother April,
When the sap begins to stir!

Take my dust and all my dreaming,
Count my heart-beats one by one,

Send them where the winters perish;
Then some golden noon recherish
And restore them in the sun,
Flower and scent and dust and dreaming,
With their heart-beats every one!

That poem is sufficient in itself to prove that Bliss Carman has full right and title to be called Spring's own lyrist, though it may be remarked here that not all his spring poems are so unfeignedly joyous. Many of them indeed, have a touch, or more than a touch, of wistfulness, for the poet knows well that sorrow lurks under all joy, deep and well hidden though it may be.

Mr. Carman sings equally finely, though perhaps not so frequently, of summer and the other seasons; but as he has other claims upon our attention, I shall forbear to labor the fact, particularly as the following collection demonstrates it sufficiently. One of those other claims is as a writer of sea poetry. Few poets, it may be said, have pictured the majesty and the mystery, the beauty and the terror of the sea, better than he. His Ballads of Lost Haven is a veritable treasure-house for those whose spirits find kinship in wide expanses of moving waters. One of the best known poems in this volume is "The Gravedigger," which opens thus:

Oh, the shambling sea is a sexton old,
And well his work is done.
With an equal grave for lord and knave,
He buries them every one.

Then hoy and rip, with a rolling hip,
He makes for the nearest shore;
And God, who sent him a thousand ship,
Will send him a thousand more;
But some he'll save for a bleaching grave,
And shoulder them in to shore—
Shoulder them in, shoulder them in,
Shoulder them in to shore.

In "The City of the Sea" (Last Songs from Vagabondia) Mr. Carman speaks of the seabells sounding

The eternal cadence of sea sorrow
For Man's lot and immemorial wrong—
The lost strains that haunt the human dwelling
With the ghost of song.

Elsewhere he speaks of

The great sea, mystic and musical.

And here from another poem is a striking picture:

... the old sea
Seems to whimper and deplore

Mourning like a childless crone
With her sorrow left alone—
The eternal human cry
To the heedless passer-by.

I have said above that Mr. Carman has had three distinct periods, and intimated that the poems in the following collection are of his third period. The first period may be said to be represented by the Low Tide and Behind the Arras volumes, while the second is displayed in the three volumes of Songs from Vagabondia, which he published in association with his friend Richard Hovey. Bliss Carman was from the first too original and individual a poet to be directly influenced by anyone else; but there can be no doubt that his friendship with Hovey helped to turn him from over-preoccupation with mysteries which, for all their greatness, are not for man to solve, to an intenser realisation of the beauty and loveliness of the world about him and of the joys of human fellowship. The result is seen in such poems as "Spring Song," quoted in part above, and his perhaps equally well-known "The Joys of the Road," which appeared in the same volume with that poem, and a few verses from which follow:

Now the joys of the road are chiefly these:
A crimson touch on the hardwood trees;

A vagrant's morning wide and blue,
In early fall, when the wind walks, too;

A shadowy highway cool and brown,
Alluring up and enticing down

From rippled waters and dappled swamp,
From purple glory to scarlet pomp;

The outward eye, the quiet will,
And the striding heart from hill to hill.

Some of the finest of arman's work is contained in his elegiac or memorial poems, in which he commemorates Keats, Shelley, William Blake, Lincoln, Stevenson, and other men for whom he has a kindred feeling, and also friends whom he has loved and lost. Listen to these moving lines from "Non Omnis Moriar," written in memory of Gleeson White, and to be found in Last Songs from Vagabondia:

There is a part of me that knows,
Beneath incertitude and fear,
I shall not perish when I pass
Beyond mortality's frontier;

But greatly having joyed and grieved,
Greatly content, shall hear the sigh
Of the strange wind across the lone
Bright lands of taciturnity.

In patience therefore I await
My friend's unchanged benign regard,—

Some April when I too shall be
Spilt water from a broken shard.

In "The White Gull," written for the centenary of the birth of Shelley in 1892, and included in By the Aurelian Wall, he thus apostrophizes that clear and shining spirit:

O captain of the rebel host,
Lead forth and far!
Thy toiling troopers of the night
Press on the unavailing fight;
The sombre field is not yet lost,
With thee for star.

Thy lips have set the hail and haste
Of clarions free
To bugle down the wintry verge
Of time forever, where the surge
Thunders and trembles on a waste
And open sea.

In "A Seamark," a threnody for Robert Louis Stevenson, which appears in the same volume, the poet hails "R.L.S." (of whose tribe he may be said to be truly one) as

The master of the roving kind,

and goes on:

O all you hearts about the world
In whom the truant gypsy blood,
Under the frost of this pale time,
Sleeps like the daring sap and flood
That dreams of April and reprieve!
You whom the haunted vision drives,
Incredulous of home and ease.
Perfection's lovers all your lives!

You whom the wander-spirit loves
To lead by some forgotten clue
Forever vanishing beyond
Horizon brinks forever new;
Our restless loved adventurer,
On secret orders come to him,
Has slipped his cable, cleared the reef,
And melted on the white sea-rim.

"Perfection's lovers all your lives." Of these, it may be said without qualification, is Bliss Carman himself.

No summary of Mr. Carman's work, however cursory, would be worthy of the name if it omitted mention of his ventures in the realm of Greek myth. From the Book of Myths is made up of work of that sort, every poem in it being full of the beauty of phrase and melody of which Mr. Carman alone has the secret. The finest poems in the book, barring the opening one, "Overlord," are "Daphne," "The Dead Faun," "Hylas," and "At Phædra's Tomb," but I can do no more here than name them, for extracts would fail to reveal their full beauty. And beauty, after all is said, is the first and last thing with Mr. Carman. As he says himself somewhere:

The joy of the hand that hews for beauty
Is the dearest solace under the sun.

And again

The eternal slaves of beauty
Are the masters of the world.

A slave—a happy, willing slave—to beauty is the poet himself, and the world can never repay him for the message of beauty which he has brought it.

Kindred to From the Book of Myths, but much more important, is Sappho: One Hundred Lyrics, one of the most successful of the numerous attempts which have been made to recapture the poems by that high priestess of song which remain to us only in fragments. Mr. Carman, as Charles G. D. Roberts points out in an introduction to the volume, has made no attempt here at translation or paraphrasing; his venture has been "the most perilous and most alluring in the whole field of poetry"—that of imaginative and, at the same time, interpretive construction. Brief quotation again would fail to convey an adequate idea of the exquisiteness of the work, and all I can do, therefore, is to urge all lovers of real poetry to possess themselves of Sappho: One Hundred Lyrics, for it is literally a storehouse of lyric beauty.

I must not fail here to speak of From the Book of Valentines, which contains some lovely things, notably "At the Great Release." This is not only one of the finest of all Mr. Carman's poems, but it is also one of the finest poems of our time. It is a love poem, and no one possessing any real feeling for poetry can read it without experiencing that strange thrill of the spirit which only the highest form of poetry can communicate. "Morning and Evening," "In an Iris Meadow," and "A letter from Lesbos" must be also mentioned. In the last named poem, Sappho is represented as writing to Gorgo, and expresses herself in these moving words:

If the high gods in that triumphant time
Have calendared no day for thee to come
Light-hearted to this doorway as of old,
Unmoved I shall behold their pomps go by—
The painted seasons in their pageantry,
The silvery progressions of the moon,
And all their infinite ardors unsubdued,
Pass with the wind replenishing the earth

Incredulous forever I must live
And, once thy lover, without joy behold,

The gradual uncounted years go by,
Sharing the bitterness of all things made.

Mention must be now made of Songs of the Sea Children, which can be described only as a collection of the sweetest and tenderest love lyrics written in our time—

—the lyric songs
The earthborn children sing,
When wild-wood laughter throngs
The shy bird-throats of spring;
When there's not a joy of the heart
But flies like a flag unfurled,
And the swelling buds bring back
The April of the world.

So perfect and complete are these lyrics that it would be almost sacrilege to quote any of them unless entire. Listen however, to these verses:

The day is lost without thee,
The night has not a star.
Thy going is an empty room
Whose door is left ajar.

Depart: it is the footfall
Of twilight on the hills.
Return: and every rood of ground
Breaks into daffodils.

There are those who will have it that Bliss Carman has been away from Canada so long that he has ceased to be, in a real sense, a Canadian. Such assume rather than know, for a very little study of his work would show them that it is shot through and through with the poet's feeling for the land of his birth. Memories of his childhood and youthful years down by the sea are still fresh in Mr. Carman's mind, and inspire him again and again in his writing. "A Remembrance," at the beginning of the present collection, may be pointed to as a striking instance of this, but proof positive is the volume, Songs from a Northern Garden, for it could have been written only by a Canadian, born and bred, one whose heart and soul thrill to the thought of Canada. I would single out from this volume for special mention as being "Canadian" in the fullest sense "In a Grand Pré Garden," "The Keeper's Silence," "At Home and Abroad," "Killoleet," and "Above the Gaspereau," but have no space to quote from them.

But Mr. Carman is not only a Canadian, he is also a Briton; and evidence of this is his Ode on the Coronation, written on the occasion of the crowning of King Edward VII in 1902. This poem—the very existence of which is hardly known among us—ought to be put in the hands of every child and youth who speaks the English tongue, for no other, I dare maintain—nothing by Kipling, or Newbolt, or any other of our so-called "Imperial singers"—expresses more truly and more movingly the deep feeling of love and reverence which the very thought of England evokes in every son of hers, even though it may never have been his to see her white cliffs rise or to tread her storied ground:

O England, little mother by the sleepless Northern tide,

Having bred so many nations to devotion, trust, and pride,
Very tenderly we turn
With welling hearts that yearn
Still to love you and defend you,—let the sons of men discern
Wherein your right and title, might and majesty, reside.

In concluding this, I greatly fear, lamentably inadequate study, I come to the collection which follows, and which, as intimated above, represents the work of Mr. Carman's latest period. I must say at once that, while I yield to no one in admiration for Low Tide and the other books of that period, or for the work of the second period, as represented by the Songs from Vagabondia volumes, I have no hesitation in declaring that I regard the poet's work of the past few years with even higher admiration. It may not possess the force and vigor of the work which preceded it; but anything seemingly missing in that respect is more than made up for me by increased beauty and clarity of expression. The mysticism—verging, or more than verging, at times on symbolism—which marked his earlier poems, and which hung, as it were, as a veil between them and the reader, has gone, and the poet's thought or theme now lies clearly before us as in a mirror. What—to take a verse from the following pages at random—could be more pellucid, more crystal clear in expression—what indeed, could come closer to that achieving of the impossible at which every real poet must aim—than this from "In Gold Lacquer".

Gold are the great trees overhead,
And gold the leaf-strewn grass,
As though a cloth of gold were spread
To let a seraph pass.
And where the pageant should go by,
Meadow and wood and stream,
The world is all of lacquered gold,
Expectant as a dream.

The poet, happily, has fully recovered from the serious illness which laid him low some two years ago, and which for a time caused his friends and admirers the gravest concern, and so we may look forward hopefully to seeing further volumes of verse come from the press to make certain his name and fame. But if, for any reason, this should not be—which the gods forfend!—Later Poems, I dare affirm, must and will be regarded as the fine flower and crowning achievement of the genius and art of Bliss Carman.

R. H. HATHAWAY.
Toronto, 1921.

Bliss Carman – A Short Biography

William Bliss Carman was born in Fredericton, in New Brunswick on April 15th 1861. 'Bliss' was his mother's maiden name. She was descended from Daniel Bliss of Concord, Massachusetts, who was the great-grandfather to Ralph Waldo Emerson.

Carman was educated at Fredericton Collegiate School. Here, under the influence of the headmaster George Robert Parkin, he gained an appreciation of classical literature and was introduced to the poetry of many of the Pre-Raphaelites especially Dante Gabriel Rossetti and Algernon Charles Swinburne.

From here he graduated to the University of New Brunswick, obtaining his B.A. there in 1881. As is common with so many writers his first published piece was for the University magazine and for Carman that was in 1879.

England now beckoned and he spent a year at Oxford and then the University of Edinburgh (1882–1883). He returned home to Canada to work on his M.A. which he obtained from the University of New Brunswick in 1884.

Tragically his father died in January, 1885, followed by his mother in February of the following year. Carman now enrolled in Harvard University for a year. There he met and was part of a literary circle that included the American poet Richard Hovey, who would become his close friend, and later collaborator, on the successful Vagabondia poetry series. Carman and Hovey were members of the "Visionists" circle along with Herbert Copeland and F. Holland Day, who would later form the Boston publishing firm Copeland & Day and, in turn, launch Vagabondia.

After Harvard Carman briefly returned to Canada, but was back in Boston by February of 1890 saying "Boston is one of the few places where my critical education and tastes could be of any use to me in earning money. New York and London are about the only other places." However, he was unable to find work in Boston but was more successful in New York becoming the literary editor of the semi-religious New York Independent. There he helped Canadian poets get published and introduced them to a wider readership than they could receive in Canada.

However, Carman and work as an editor were not destined for a long career together and he was dismissed in 1892. There followed short stays with Current Literature, Cosmopolitan, The Chap-Book, and The Atlantic Monthly. Whilst these appointments provided the basis for a career and an income he was not suited to their demands. From 1895 he would only work as a contributor to magazines and newspapers whilst he worked on his volumes of poetry.

Carman first published a book of poetry in 1893 with Low Tide on Grand Pré. He had written the title poem in the summer of 1886 and it had (whilst he was still at Harvard) been published in the spring of 1887 by Atlantic Monthly. Despite its critical acceptance there was no Canadian company prepared to publish the volume. When an American company did so it went bankrupt. Life was becoming difficult for the young poet.

The following year was decidedly better. His partnership with Richard Hovey had given birth to Songs of Vagabondia and it was published by their friends at Copeland & Day. It was an immediate success. The young men were delighted at such a reception. It quickly sold out and was re-printed a number of times. Although these re-prints were small (usually 500-1000 copies) they were frequent.

On the back of this success they would write a further three volumes, which in their turn were almost as successful. They quickly became the center of a cult following, especially among students who empathized with the poetry's anti-materialistic themes, its celebration of personal freedom, and its glorification of comradeship."

The success of Songs of Vagabondia prompted the Boston firm, Stone & Kimball, to reissue Low Tide on Grand Pré and to hire Carman as the editor of its literary journal, The Chapbook. This ceased after a year when the company relocated and Carman expressed his desire to remain in Boston.

In 1885 Carman brought out Behind the Arras, a somewhat more serious and philosophical work centered on the premise of a long meditation using the speaker's house and its many rooms as a symbol of life and the choices to be made. However, the idea and its execution did not quite meld.

Signficantly, in 1896, Carman met Mrs Mary Perry King, who rapidly became patron, adviser and sometime lover. She put money in his pocket, and food in his mouth and, when he struck bottom, often repaired his confidence as well as helping to sell the work. She also later became his writing collaborator on two verse dramas.

Mitchell Kennerley, Carman's roommate wrote that, "On the rare occasions they had intimate relations they always advised me of by leaving a bunch of violets — Mary favorite flower — on the pillow of my bed." If her husband, Dr. King, knew of this arrangement he seems not to have objected. He was a great supporter of Carman's career and seemingly his wife's complicated involvement with that.

In 1897 Carman published Ballad of Lost Haven, a collection of poetry about the sea. Its notable poems include the macabre sea shanty, The Gravedigger. The following year, 1898, came By the Aurelian Wall, the title poem itself was an elegy to John Keats and the book a collection of formal elegies.

In 1899 his publisher, Lamson, Wolffe was taken over by the Boston firm of Small, Maynard & Co., who had also acquired the rights to Low Tide on Grand Pré. The copyrights to of his books were now held by one publisher and, in lieu of earnings, Carman took what would ultimately be a disastrous financial stake in the company.

As the century turned Carman was hard at work on what would eventually be a five-volume set of poetry; "Pans Pipes". Pan, the goat-god, was traditionally associated with poetry and the coming together of the earthly and the divine. The five volumes were all published between 1902 – 1905.

The inspiration for this came from Mary who had persuaded Carman to write in both prose and poetry about the ideas of 'unitrinianism.' This drew on the theories of François-Alexandre-Nicolas-Chéri Delsarte and was defined as a strategy of mind-body-spirit harmonization aimed at undoing the physical, psychological, and spiritual damage caused by urban modernity. The definition may be rather woolly but for Carman it resulted in some very fine work across the five-volume series. This shared belief between Mary and Carman created a further bond but did isolate him from his circle of friends.

The excellence of a number of these poems did much to install Carman as the most noted of Canadian Poets and eventually their own Poet Laureate. Among the most often quoted and printed are "The Dead Faun" (from Volume I), "Lord of My Heart's Elation" (Volume II) and many of the erotic poems from Volume III.

In the middle of publication in 1903, Small, Maynard failed and with it went all the assets Carman had tied up in the company.

Carman immediately signed with another Boston publisher, L.C. Page, who would publish seven new books of Carman poetry in this hectic period up to 1905. They released a further three books based on Carman's Transcript columns, and a prose work on Unitrinianism, The Making of Personality, that he'd written with Mary King.

Carman now felt secure enough to pursue his 'dream project,' namely a deluxe edition of his collected poetry to 1903. Page acquired the distribution rights on the condition that the book be sold privately, by subscription. Unfortunately, the demand wasn't there and it failed. Carman was deeply disappointed and lost faith in Page. However, their grip on his copyrights was absolute and sadly no further collected editions were to be published during his lifetime.

By 1904 his income was restricted and the offer to be editor-in-chief of the 10-volume project, The World's Best Poetry, was eagerly accepted.

For Carman perhaps his best years as a poet were now behind him. From 1908 he lived near the Kings' New Canaan, Connecticut, estate, that he named "Sunshine", or in the summer in a cabin in the Catskills, which he called "Moonshine."

With Literary tastes now moving away from what he could provide his income further dwindled and his health started to deteriorate.

In 1912 Carman published the final work in the Vagabondia series. Richard Hovey had died in 1900 and so this last work was purely his. It has a distinct elegiac tone as if remembering the past works themselves.

Although Carman was not politically active he did campaign during the World War One, as a member of the Vigilantes, who supported the American entry into the titanic struggle on the Allied side.

By 1920, Carman was impoverished and recovering from a near-fatal attack of tuberculosis. He returned to Canada and began to undertake a series of publicly successful and somewhat lucrative reading tours, saying "there is nothing worth talking of in book sales compared with reading. Breathless attention, crowded halls, and a strange, profound enthusiasm such as I never guessed could be,' he reported to a friend. 'And good thrifty money too. Think of it! An entirely new life for me, and I am the most surprised person in Canada.'"

On October 28th, 1921 Carman was honored at a dinner held by the newly-formed Canadian Authors' Association, at the Ritz Carlton Hotel in Montreal, where he was crowned Canada's Poet Laureate with a wreath of maple leaves.

Carman is placed among the Confederation Poets, a group that included his cousin, Charles G.D. Roberts, Archibald Lampman, and Duncan Campbell Scott. Carman was perhaps the best and is credited with the widest recognition. However, whilst the others carefully supplemented their income with writing novels and works for the magazines, or even other careers, Carman only wrote poetry together with a small amount of writing on literary ideas, philosophy, and aesthetics.

He continued his reading tours, and by 1925 had finally secured a new Canadian publisher; McClelland & Stewart (Toronto), who issued a collection of selected earlier verse and would now became his main publisher. Although they benefited from Carman's increased popularity and his revered position in Canadian literature, his former publisher L.C. Page would not relinquish its copyrights to his earlier works.

In his last years, Carman was a member of the Halifax literary and social set, The Song Fishermen and in 1927 he edited The Oxford Book of American Verse.

William Bliss Carman died of a brain hemorrhage, at the age of 68, in New Canaan on the 8th June, 1929. He was cremated in New Canaan and his ashes interred at Forest Hill Cemetery, Fredericton, with a national memorial service held at the Anglican cathedral there.

It was only a quarter of a century later, on May 13th, 1954, that a scarlet maple tree was planted at his graveside, to honour his request in the 1892 poem "The Grave-Tree":

Let me have a scarlet maple
For the grave-tree at my head,
With the quiet sun behind it,
In the years when I am dead.

Bliss Carman – A Concise Bibliography

Poetry Collections
Low Tide on Grand Pre: A Book of Lyrics (1893)
Songs from Vagabondia (1894)
A Seamark: A Threnody for Robert Louis Stevenson (1895)
Behind the Arras: A Book of the Unseen (1895)
More Songs from Vagabondia (1896)
Ballads of Lost Haven: A Book of the Sea (1897)
By the Aurelian Wall: And Other Elegies (1898)
A Winter Holiday (1899)
Last Songs from Vagabondia (1901)
Ballads and Lyrics (1902)
Ode on the Coronation of King Edward (1902)
Pipes of Pan: From the Book of Myths (1902)
Pipes of Pan: From the Green Book of the Bards (1903)
Pipes of Pan: Songs of the Sea Children (1904)
Pipes of Pan: Songs from a Northern Garden (1904)
Pipes of Pan: From the Book of Valentines (1905)
Sappho: One Hundred Lyrics (1904)
Poems (1905)
The Rough Rider: And Other Poems (1909)
A Painter's Holiday, and Other Poems (1911)
Echoes from Vagabondia (1912)
April Airs: A Book of New England Lyrics (1916)
The Man of The Marne: And Other Poems (1918)
The Vengeance of Noel Brassard: A Tale of the Acadian Expulsion (1919)
Far Horizons (1925)
Later Poems (1926)
Sanctuary: Sunshine House Sonnets (1929)
Wild Garden (1929)
Bliss Carman's Poems (1931)

Drama

Bliss Carman & Mary Perry King. Daughters of Dawn: A Lyrical Pageant of a Series of Historical Scenes for Presentation with Music and Dancing (1913)

Bliss Carman & Mary Perry King. Earth Deities: And Other Rhythmic Masques (1914)

Prose Collections

The Kinship of Nature (1904)

The Poetry of Life (1905)

The Friendship of Art (1908)

The Making of Personality (1908)

Talks on Poetry and Life; Being a Series of Five Lectures Delivered Before the University of Toronto, December 1925 (Speech). transcribed by Blanche Hume. 1926.

Bliss Carman's Scrap-Book: A Table of Contents (Pierce, Lorne, editor) (1931)

Editor

The World's Best Poetry (10 volumes) (1904)

The Oxford Book of American Verse (U.S. editor) (1927)

Carman, Bliss; Pierce, Lorne, editors (1935). Our Canadian Literature: Representative Verse, English and French.

www.ingramcontent.com/pod-product-compliance
Lightning Source LLC
Chambersburg PA
CBHW070108070426
42448CB00038B/2329